DAISY'S TREATS

Finding the Courage to Love Unconditionally

"When I feel love, I feel peace beyond all understanding.
When I feel love, nothing else matters."
~Daisy

Artwork and Book Design by Jenifer Novak Landers
All rights reserved. Permission to reproduce any selection from this book
must be granted in writing from the publisher.

Published in the United States by
Fully Inspired Publishing.
www.fullyinspiredpublishing.com
The text of this book is set in Cambria.
Library of Congress Catalogue-in-Publication Data is on file.
ISBN 978-1-953978-04-2

Daisy's Treats is dedicated to humans who want more love, gratitude and peace.

"A dog is the only thing on earth that loves you more than he loves himself."

~Josh Billings (humorist)

Contents

A Full Year of Daisy's Wisdom
52 Weekly Devotions

Introduction

When I adopted Daisy from a rescue, I had no idea she would inspire me to create a book!

This adventure began on Facebook, without me realizing it.

As a new dog owner, I saturated my Facebook page with photos of Daisy, including the channeled wisdom with each corresponding photo. My audience was loving the posts and looked forward to more.

I was told by many of my Facebook friends that I should put these "devotions" into a book, and so it began.

I had a "conversation" with Daisy where she challenged me. She suggested we write "Daisy's Treats". My fearful ego went into resistance, thinking it would be stupid, or people would think I'm crazy, and the list of fearful thoughts and excuses goes on and on.

Clearly, my resistance was the trigger to move forward. Had I listened to my fear, I never would have taken this on. Since I teach and coach people to shift their fear into fearlessness, I knew that I must continue to model it, walk the talk, feel the fear, and do it anyway.

As you can see, there are 52 weeks of wisdom from Daisy. Each week has the same purpose, which is about *"Finding the courage to love unconditionally."*

The photos serve as metaphors, inviting you a new and deeper level of self-awareness. Self-awareness will shift your mindset, yet without application, change will not happen.

This is why I decided to add my perspective with a weekly treat, serving as a structure for you to apply the wisdom in a way that will create transformation.

I have authored several other books, and none of them came close to the joy I've experienced writing "Daisy's Treats".

Daisy has changed my life and now the change can ripple into your life. I've always had a penchant for communicating with nature, particularly the trees, birds, oceans, rivers and streams. I've always received messages of the truth from all of it. I don't believe it's due to some special gift. It's simply that I've been intentional with being in relationship with everything, as I believe everything has a spiritual nature and carries messages of great truth and value.

It was May 2nd, 2020, when this angelic being named Daisy entered my life. Since then, she has taught me to give and receive love abundantly, no matter what the situation.

The wisdom channeled through me has shifted my world from fear to love and joy. I am committed to applying Daisy's Treats and Devotions every week for the rest of my life.

*"In a gentle way,
you can shake the world."*

~Mahatma Ghandhi

Finding the Courage to Love Unconditionally

I wrote this book with the intention to help you remember that you have always had the courage to love. Unconditional love means reaching beyond anything in the way of the pure expression of love, the pure exchange of love and just honoring love as it is.

As long as you have the willingness to reach inside yourself to access it, and by applying the wisdom and coaching tips, you will realize how much more love you are capable of expressing towards yourself and everyone around you.

When I look at my purpose for writing this book, here are my values:

Finding courage within.

Learning to love unconditionally.

Loving myself and others without limits or fear.

Allowing my courage to overcome my fears.

Learning the power of LOVE.

Being the power of LOVE.

In gratitude for dogs who LOVE every moment.

How to use Weekly Devotions and Treats

Enjoy all 52 weeks at your own pace.

Your year of unconditional love starts on the date you choose to begin. Proceed with each Devotion and Treat week by week as you go along.

You may want to read through the entire book first just to enjoy the full journey with Daisy!

Keep the book handy as you create new weekly habits for yourself.

The photos serve as metaphors, inviting you to see new perspectives and open your heart to love.

"Devotions" = A personal observance of higher awareness.

Expanding your awareness will shift your mindset, yet without application, change will not happen.

This is why there are "Treats"!

As a Master Certified Coach with over 20 years' experience helping people find greater fulfillment in their lives and careers, I add my perspective with each weekly Treat. The structure of a weekly Devotion and Treat helps you apply the wisdom to create transformation.

"Treats" = A coaching perspective with actions.

Use this section to step into the level of love you are capable of expressing.

Schedule a time each day to reflect on the lesson and commit to the suggested practice of the week. If you lose focus, just allow yourself to jump back in.

This is not about perfection.

By practicing (and having fun!) with each weekly Devotion and Treat, it will ultimately move you forward into the life you most desire.

After all, we want more love, gratitude and peace.

"My wish for you is to be treated with the wisdom Daisy has shared with me, and that you apply the wisdom so you, too, can give and receive love abundantly!"

~Debbie Leoni

Daisy's Devotions
WEEK 1

When my person took this photo of me, I could tell that she was touched. I was wondering what she was thinking. Was it because I looked dog-eared to her?

Well, she must have known that I was wondering what she was wondering. She told me that there's really nothing to be said. The eyes say it all. And she told me that I reminded her to always keep one ear open, just like I'm doing in the photo.

I think she really digs me!

May you allow your eyes and ears to gift you with miracles taking place in every moment.

Your Weekly Treat

With technology being the most predominant way of
communicating, there's very little eye contact happening
these days, not to mention deep listening. Choose
someone important in your life this week to practice
making eye contact more than ever, and use your ears
to listen deeply to them. Notice how it deepens your
relationship.

If it feels uncomfortable, then you really need to practice!
Put down your phone, laptop or ipad and give someone
the greatest gift ever: Your Presence.

By the way, it will feel like a treat for you too!

Daisy's Devotions
WEEK 2

My person told me today that I'm teaching her to hold close to all that she treasures, that everything is temporary, except for love.

I have a feeling that she is going to love me forever. No wonder my tail wags so much!

May you show those you love you will love them forever.

Your Weekly Treat

Have you heard it said before that you can't take "it" with you?

What are your "its" that you may be holding onto for fulfillment and gratification? Might your "its" be money, status, things?

Spend this week reflecting on what matters most, and each day make sure you are taking at least one action that supports what matters most.

Almost always, when I ask my clients the question: "What matters most?" they answer, "family." Yet when we dig deeper into the conversation, they realize that most of the time they are spending is on the "its," the temporary. Daisy treasures the bone she's holding, yet she doesn't have to stop to realize that what matters most is not the bone. It's her devotion to her person.

Take advantage of this week to prove to yourself that what matters most is being reflected in your actions.

Daisy's Devotions
WEEK 3

Life is so full of new discoveries. Today I discovered what it's like to have a grandmother. I already feel totally loved by my person, but WOW! This is the shizz! She loves me just as my person does, and she spoils me too!

I'm not allowed on the couch, but Gramma lets me! Snuggling with her is awesome because she doesn't stop petting me.

My person doesn't let me eat people food, but Gramma does! I have a strong sense more spoiling is in store for today!!! I can't stop wagging my tail!

I can't imagine how my person can't stand the pain of being cut off from her grandkids. Those poor kids are missing out on so much love and spoiling.

I'm going to chomp onto each special moment with Gramma, especially since she's almost 91 and has cancer. My tail may be long but life is too short to let anything get in the way of being spoiled with love.

May you let go of anything that may hinder you from spoiling everyone you love, today and always.

Your Weekly Treat

I grew up believing spoiling was a bad thing!

"Oh, they spoil their kids. That kid is so spoiled!" Clearly, there was a need for healthy boundaries. But what if spoiling can be a good thing?

What if spoiling means you abundantly love yourself and everyone else? What would our world be like?

"What the world needs now, is love sweet love," sang Dionne Warwick. ".... not just for some, but for everyone."

How might you be withholding love? What are you waiting for in order to express love? Fear of rejection, unworthiness and resentment are often 3 culprits that hinder abundant love.

Start with yourself. Each day this week take at least one action to love yourself abundantly. This means you get to prove to yourself that you are worth all the love you desire. Make a list of all the ways you deny yourself love. Then do whatever it takes to cross off every item on the list. The world needs your love, sweet love!

Daisy's Devotions
WEEK 4

What's tomorrow?

I have no need to know and it's much better this way.

May you live knowing that nothing is real except for this moment.

Your Weekly Treat

Spend some time this week journaling on all the ways you are holding yourself hostage from the past and/or worrying about the future.

As you do, notice how it affects how you feel.

Then, STOP, and meditate just for 3 minutes, simply focusing on your breath, just like Daisy is doing here.

Each time you pause, you are calling yourself back home.

Daisy's Devotions
WEEK 5

I heard about this guy from the past called Buddha.

He could sit for hours! I don't know how he did it! My person is training me to sit and it's a real challenge, especially when I see a squirrel.

She's also teaching me that I don't have to sit like the Buddha to find enlightenment. Any sit will do. Even if it's for a few seconds. Enlightenment can happen in that split second that, like that split second when I see she has a treat in her hand for me.

May you find enlightenment in the most menial tasks and trust it's always available.

Your Weekly Treat

There is no one way to achieve enlightenment.

What I have found to be in the way of so many who say they want to be enlightened is their judgment around what it needs to look like.

What if enlightenment was only a split second of the sunset, or the sound of laughter? By letting go of your attachment to being enlightened, you are giving yourself access to exactly that!

Each day this week, set your alarm once in the am, once at midday and once in the late afternoon. Give yourself 1 minute to stop what you are doing and bring your attention right here and right now.

Ask yourself:

"What is enlightening about this moment?

Daisy's Devotions
WEEK 6

When I feel loved, I feel a peace that surpasses all understanding.

Maybe the peace comes from being petted, or a warm blanket enfolded around me. I just know when I feel loved, that nothing else matters. Nada. Zilch.

It feels amazing when the being you are with is loving on you, yet even when I'm alone with my toys and bones, all I need to do is remember. Love knows no space or time. It has no limits. It's always there!

May your love minister the peace that surpasses all understanding to everyone around you by simply remembering.

Your Weekly Treat

Do you think you need someone to act a certain way so you can feel loved?

Or do you think you need to achieve something in order to feel lovable?

These kinds of thoughts will have you forever chasing something that will never last until you turn inward.

- √ Pay attention this week to the energy you evoke throughout your day.

- √ Check in several times a day and identify the quality of your beingness.

- √ Then ask yourself: "What do I need to shift into love right now?" Sit with that quality. Allow it to fill up every part of you.

It takes only seconds to access love!

Daisy's Devotions
WEEK 7

My person and me can't figure out if it's my meditative demeanor or hers that seems to be rubbing off onto each of us.

I hope my peaceful spirit rubs off on all those crazy dogs who just want to fight.

Maybe you humans can do the same. I mean, really: What's the point of growling at each other?

May you follow Daisy's example of equanimity, tranquility, and peace as you move through your day.

Your Weekly Treat

Oh, to have Daisy's demeanor! Well, what's different about Daisy and us is that she rarely is in flight, fight or freeze mode. She knows there's very little to be afraid of. Her stress response is almost nil, unlike us!

Recommit to your meditation practice this week, even if it's only for a few minutes. Know that you need not sit to meditate. Walking in nature, painting, dancing: all of these are meditative practices. Commit to something that cultivates focus. By doing this, you are not only creating more calm in yourself, but for everyone around you. It's contagious!

Daisy's Devotions
WEEK 8

Who says you need to have a reason for everything you do? I know I don't. I just let the spirit move me and have fun with it. It's ok to act stupid. Wait! What's stupid mean?

My person says labels are stupid, so I'll go with that. Anyway, be like a dog today and let yourself do things without a reason. Then I can laugh at you like my person laughs at me!

May your week be filled with laughter, silliness, and a joyful spirit.

Your Weekly Treat

I can't imagine my life without silliness and laughter. Yet I find myself being much too serious. The same goes for my clients. I'll ask them when the last time was when they played or acted silly? They can't remember, yet when they reminisce about those times, their energy shifts. It's palpable!

What about you? When was the last time you couldn't stop laughing? When was the last time you played with abandon? Remember how much fun it was?

Spend some time considering what has been in the way for you. Some the reasons I hear are, "I don't want to be judged. I have too much to do, or I need to act like an adult."

Those reasons, stories and excuses are preventing you from being fully expressed and joyful!

Commit to stepping out of your comfort zone and have fun!

Daisy's Devotions
WEEK 9

Did you ever hear the saying, "Like attracts like?" Well, there are no accidents that I rescued my person because we are so similar. Check out all the ways that we mirror each other:

Allergies, not very hairy, contemplative and happy, nosy, estranged by loved ones, recovering from trauma, water fuels our soul (sitting by the water, swimming, drinking it), anxiety skyrockets when gong to the doctor/vet awaiting test results, respects boundaries (well, most of the time), can't go a day without being outside, hates noise and loves to smell things, loves being home, especially in our bed, loves people, and we're loners.

My point is: instead of wanting a loved one to change to be more like you, focus on how they already are! You will be surprised how alike you are

May you devote your life to finding oneness with everything in creation.

Your Weekly Treat

Just about every time I reflect on similarities, I become emotional. I become cognizant of all the ways that I judge others, which has me feeling disconnected and often alone. What a waste of energy when the truth is that our similarities outweigh our differences.

Who's the person in your life who you most struggle with? It may be someone you are very close to, or it may be someone outside of your social circle, such as a politician, leader, etc. Give yourself time this week to consider all the ways that you and the other person are similar. I bet you'll be surprised!

Then close your eyes and imagine that person is sitting across from you. As you connect with them, focus on the similarities. Practice this each day this week, and as you do, reflect on how your feelings towards this other person is shifting. Enjoy the oneness!

Daisy's Devotions
WEEK 10

I never would have allowed myself to lie on my back this way the first day I was rescued.

I get lots of kisses and snuggles when I'm totally vulnerable. It has me feeling especially close to my person and it seems like her body softens when it happens.

There's nothing ruff about that!

May your most raw, authentic self be expressed in a way that fosters intimacy, connection, and deep love.

Your Weekly Treat

The times in my life when I've chosen to bust through my fear and reveal my most real self are the times when I've felt most connected to others and they to me. Vulnerability is the greatest measurement of courage! And it offers such abundant rewards.

Who's someone you'd love to become closer with? I can assure you that by being vulnerable, things will shift. Notice the fear that has prevented you from delivering a message or communicating from your most vulnerable self? Imagine what you would say to this person if you had no fear? How would you say it? Then, put it on paper. Practice delivering the message. Last, and not least, do it!

Daisy's Devotions
WEEK 11

I don't have much to say today except that my person tells me she wakes up with a smile every day because of me. Chew on that for a while.

May your beingness become like a light in the darkness, shining the truth of the universe.

Your Weekly Treat

Several times during my day, I'll step away from my desk or whatever else I'm doing, and lay close to my girl, Daisy. No matter how anxious I feel, she brings me calm. Imagine being that for someone?

It's easy to forget how much our mood affects others. Think of a time when you walked into a room with a very negative person. How did it feel? I know I can feel it and it can be a challenge to remain grounded and calm in their midst. The reverse scenario is just as impactful. Have you ever walked into a room with someone who IS the light? Need I say more?

This week, use a sticky note or any kind of reminder to help you choose the mood that best serves you. Others will be pleased!

Daisy's Devotions
WEEK 12

Did you know that one of the reasons why I curl up in a ball like this when I sleep comes from my ancestors? I suppose it's in my genes. Anyway, I do it because in the olden days, we did this to create warmth and to protect my most vulnerable organs from possible predators. Oh, how they would have loved a cozy, warm crate like mine!

I know I've inherited lots of other behaviors and I don't get too squirrelly about figuring them out because all of it makes me who I am.

Who I am is not just what you see. I am my descendants and I honor the intrinsic intelligence which exists in me because of them.

p.s. My words above made my mom emotional as she sits here with me thinking of her ancestors and the gratitude she has for the ways they sculpted her into knowing abundant love. And she's especially happy that she has her very own person house that keeps her safe and warm.

May your memory be recalled daily of the values, traditions, and codes your ancestors provided you to live your fullest life, and honor the gift of life which has been passed on to you.

Your Weekly Treat

Either have a conversation with a family member or journal using the following questions:

What are some of the traditions that have been passed on to me?

Who passed them on to me and how did they influence what I believe?

How have these traditions and customs impacted who I am today?

What new practice or practices will I establish to remain grounded in my traditions?

Then, make sure you are staying grounded in these traditions so you, too, can pass them down.

Daisy's Devotions
WEEK 13

She's tall, I'm short

I have a tail and for the life of me she can't find hers.

She has 2 teats. I have 9.

Her hands smell like roses. My paws smell like Fritos.

Since I'm a dog, I don't focus on our differences. at. all. So why would anyone be so dogged to hound on the things that have you feeling separate from another?

Look at our eyes in this photo. Pause, and notice that both sets are windows to our souls. Enter in and notice that in our soul space, there's only sameness; oneness, harmony.

That's why I love staring at her. When I do, it doesn't matter that her hands don't smell like Fritos. I don't judge her for having only 2 teats. The soul space is where love happens, always.

May you allow your eyes to open the windows to your soul space. Let us in, because we all reside there.

Your Weekly Treat

In this crazy era of technology, eye contact has almost become a thing of the past.

When I lead workshops, often I have the attendees partake in an exercise where they practice communicating (listening and speaking) with only their eyes. The depth of insight and connection that happens is clearly beyond words. For many of the participants, they become quite uncomfortable, because it requires vulnerability. They walk away with a new willingness to be vulnerable with those they love.

Notice this week how often you are making eye contact with the one you are communicating with. Make a concerted effort to communicate with your eyes more than your mouth. Then share with them what shifted because of it. You will be pleased!

Daisy's Devotions
WEEK 14

FYI, you don't have to be a kid to have an imaginary friend.

You can see in this photo, that I'm whispering secrets to my cuddly friend here. It's completely safe to share my deepest secrets with her and she just listens without trying to fix me, judge me or make me wrong in any way.

Other than my person, I feel really close to my imaginary bff. Kind of crazy how I can have such an intimate relationship with something that is not real!

My person is teaching me that everything in life is imaginary. That sort of blows my mind when I think about it. She says that our mind imagines everything and that life is an illusion, even though it doesn't make sense.

I'm hoping you humans will really get what I'm saying: that you can use your imagination to live your life with lots of happiness like me!

May you embrace the whimsical part of you and imagine something that delivers a level of enjoyment, intimacy, and playfulness!

Your Weekly Treat

Did you ever have a pretend friend when you were a kid? I had an imaginary king that sat on top my dresser. I could see him and at nighttime, we would talk to each other. He made me feel safe in the darkness.

I told my mom about the king and she thought it was cute. Yet she would chuckle about it, sending me the message that he wasn't real.

I made the king real, and that's what mattered. Herein lies the gift of our imagination. If you think about it, everything we think comes from our imagination. We've all chosen to be authors of a fictional narrative about life.

So why not use your imagination to create a life that will shift your experience into what you desire?

Who or what can you invite into your imagination that will enhance your connection to self and the world? Remember, it's all made up!

This week allow yourself to access the quality of a child; the child who innately knows how to use their imagination to feel safety, joy, playfulness, and connection.

Daisy's Devotions
WEEK 15

Don't tell her I told you, but my person still worries too much. Most of the time, she's usually chill, but she still worries about getting sick. She worries that she will die alone, that our country will never be united, and all this other rabid stuff that I can't come close to understanding in my canine brain.

I don't think she realizes how much I can feel her worry and anxiety.

Here's what's magical about the power I never knew I had: I suppose I have some sort of doggie instinct that gives me the ability to positively impact everyone around me. I'll go up and snuggle with her and I can feel her heart melt.

She told me that when this happens, her reality becomes better than her dreams. Now THAT is one humongous treat!

May your magical abilities cause someone's reality to be better than their dreams.

Your Weekly Treat

When was the last time you knew you were bringing calm to a loved one just by your presence?

Life isn't just about us, even though it's easy to feel this way. What if you could commit this week to being a calming presence to everyone around you?

Here's what I invite you to do this week: Consider what you must let go of in order to positively impact someone else. Spend three minutes before you interact, using your breath to become grounded. Then bring this energy into your relationships and notice the impact you are making, not only on them but with yourself!

Daisy's Devotions
WEEK 16

What I've learned in my 3'ish (no one knows for sure how old I am) years of life, is that I don't always have to be in the driver's seat.

Being in the back seat offers me oodles of benefits.

I get to completely enjoy the ride, trusting that wherever I'm being carried will be safe.

Being in the back seat has me fancy the notion that I rarely have to be the driver. I mean, yeah, I need to decide where I'm going to poop and pee, but really, by staying put in the back seat, it can relieve me of all the ways I get anxious and scared.

May you be the passenger to what drives you towards the highest good, and enjoy the ride.

Your Weekly Treat

Isn't it exhausting to always feel like you need to be in control of everything? It is for me, so as a "recovering control freak," I've learned to surrender to "what is" more than ever. Because of it, my life has changed dramatically towards ease, peace, and acceptance.

It takes a conscious commitment to do the work daily.

Journal this week, (By the way, if you are not one who likes to journal, another powerful alternative is to speak into a recorder and play it back to yourself. Really cool!), about all the things you are trying to control. The need to control is a fear-based coping mechanism that has us feeling as if we are in charge, yet it only leads to exhaustion, frustration, and often resentment.

As you journal, include the reasons why you are trying to control something or someone. Then continue writing about what will be possible by busting through your fear. Remember, when we are trying to control, we are making it about us. When we release our fear and let go, we are making it about the we.

Daisy's Devotions
WEEK 17

Gramma is leaving today. I'm trying to hold on. I guess I'm more human than I thought. It sort of makes sense. Why wouldn't I want to hold onto something so good? I mean, think about it! If she was around all the time, I'd be licking dishes daily! What a dream that would be! I'd never be in the doghouse when she's around!

You know what? Maybe holding on is a good thing sometimes. It's ok.

When she's gone, I can bask in the memories with her and be pleased.

May you hold onto all that is love and let go of everything that is not.

Your Weekly Treat

I have so many wonderful memories with my grandparents, special friends, and family members, and I would imagine you do, too. The events and circumstances are in the past, yet there is also a fullness beyond what is temporal. What you are left with are feelings of love, which keep us feeling full. All we need to do is pause and remember. When you remember, we lose our sense of time and land in a space which takes us into intimacy with the beloved.

This week: Gift yourself by claiming the moments in your life that you most want to hold onto, as Daisy does. Meditate on these people in your life. Bring them into your awareness. Remove any boundaries of space and time and enjoy the depths of love available in the moment.

Daisy's Devotions
WEEK 18

No matter what the situation, I know that one of my richest treasures is my personal dignity. And I didn't have to learn that in training class. It just comes with the package of who I am.

Even the strongest undercurrent cannot rob me of my dignity, so stand strong and tall like I do! Even if you need to dog paddle your way through, you can do it with dignity!

May you rise above the undercurrent in your life to stand tall.

Your Weekly Treat

Why is it that we tend to lose our dignity based on external circumstances? Perhaps someone has denigrated you, offered you what we consider negative feedback, or hurt you in some way.

You get to choose your dignity, no matter what the undercurrent happening outside of you.

Every day this week, stand in front of a mirror. Choose your most powerful posture, as if you are a superhero. Notice how it changes your state into the highest version of yourself. Use this posture to show up with the dignity you know you have.

And remember: Sticks and stones can break your bones, but you choose whether words will hurt you!

Daisy's Devotions
WEEK 19

What the ......???

This is some scary sh..t! I've never seen anything like this! Yes, I was afraid, yet I also had a sense of curiosity with what was in front of me! So instead of backing away, I acquiesced to my curiosity.

What I realized is that my fear is a primal instinct; a natural survival mechanism that warns me of potential danger, and that's a good thing.

There's rarely ANYTHING to be afraid of!

I can take those ghosts and goblins on any day! But I won't, because they are cute and funny.

And they remind me that I am fearless! Hey, that's the name of my person's book! I Am Fearless: 12 Elements of Fearless Living. (She told me to plug that in.)

Now if I can only get over my fear of that scary, big German Shepherd across the street, you might be able to see a photo of both of us together.

May your curiosity conquer your fear, and may you befriend the ghosts and goblins that show up in your life!

Your Weekly Treat

Daisy nailed it when she said, "There's rarely anything to be afraid of." Fear is very real, but only seldom. Most of the time it's an internal narrative which puts us into flight, fight or freeze mode. Fear is an emotion which is driven by your thoughts. The only difference between fear and excitement is your perspective.

Daisy instinctively knew to stop and notice that she had nothing to be afraid of, which is what shifted her experience. You can do the same if you are willing to practice.

What's your fear? Failure, rejection, abandonment, conflict? This week, identify what you are most afraid of. Spend time journaling around the fictional narrative you have authored that has you afraid. Write about what the fear is costing you; how it affects your stress level, your sense of peace and joy.

Next, consider what support or resources you need to shift your fear into fearlessness. You need not do this alone, and the resources are abundant.

Last, feel the fear and do it anyway.

Daisy's Devotions
WEEK 20

WARNING: This photo is R rated due to nudity.

My person was worried that I wouldn't like my first bath at home. Ha! Little did she know how much I loved it. (She really needs to stop gnawing on so many worries!)

The water was warm, she scrubbed me with gentleness, playfulness, and lots of TLC, making sure I didn't get soap in my eyes.

It wasn't so much the act of bathing per se. It was the loving attention she gave me that felt so yummy, bubbly, and restorative.

In our nakedness together, we became immersed in a loving togetherness of giving and receiving.

By the way, the bath water wasn't very dirty!

May you feel worthy to share your most naked self with everyone around you and bathe in the intimate love available.

Your Weekly Treat

"I won't be loved if my shadows are exposed. I won't be accepted if they know my secrets; my sins, and the desperate longings that I hide. If I'm completely naked, my imperfections will be exposed which means I will be rejected."

I have yet to meet anyone who hasn't had these thoughts and others similar. It seems that we believe if we put all our energy into showing up perfectly - then we will be accepted. As Dr. Phil would say, "How's that working?"

This week, imagine what you could experience if you removed the veil of illusion you show the world, and allow yourself complete emotional freedom by being fully expressed? If it feels scary, then know that you are being called to a greater expression of you. This expression of you can and will dramatically cultivate a level of love that you most likely never experienced.

Think about it. Don't you want your loved ones to do the same? It must happen within yourself first. Take off your mask. It's not working. Today is the day.

Get naked.

Daisy's Devotions
WEEK 21

Last night was hell. Yesterday I ate something I shouldn't have and clearly it didn't agree with my little tummy. I listened to my gut instinct because I knew to vomit it out and I did more than once.

The pain was awful for a while. As I shivered and cried, my person did this thing called Reiki on my tummy, and the pain finally disappeared, just like my bones disappear after I hide them.

My person's hands made me feel safe and nurtured. She told me my cortisol levels were going down and my oxytocin was going up. She tells me things I don't understand but the tone of her soft voice had me sure it was good. That's when the healing happened. Love heals.

May you soften someone's pain with human touch, and feel your heart open in a way that heals the pain of the world.

Your Weekly Treat

Did you know that there are studies showing that touch signals safety, trust, and it soothes? Basic warm touch calms cardiovascular stress. It activates the body's Vagus nerve, which is intimately involved with our compassionate response, and a simple touch can trigger release of oxytocin, aka "the love hormone."

You innately know how to do this. Here's an example. Imagine you tripped and landed on your elbow. What's the first thing you do? I bet you put your opposite hand on your elbow to comfort it. Touch heals and you need not be a Reiki practitioner to heal with touch.

This week, use your gift of touch on yourself. Perhaps try meditating with your hand on your heart or on any part of your body that feels tense. Remember to touch those around you, with their permission. And trust you have the power to heal.

Daisy's Devotions
WEEK 22

The night before last, my person abundantly loved on me during an atrocious belly ache. Her love healed me.

Well, the reverse happened yesterday. Her pain wasn't in her belly. She had one of those days where she felt very out of sorts; anxious, and depressed over the collective chaos happening in the world.

I snuggled up to her very close and simply offered my doggie presence.

It felt like she melted so much that we became one being. She smiled into me. I had no clue how much I could help her. I healed her just by doing what I know best: love.

May your love be an unconscious response to everything and everyone.

Your Weekly Treat

The soul knows what to do, always. The ego is what gets in the way because the ego needs to self-identify with control, fixing, managing, and lies.

What if you could let go of effort? Deepak Chopra states in "The Seven Spiritual Laws of Success," "Attention to the ego consumes the greatest amount of energy."

Thinking is exhausting!

This week, might you create a daily practice (maybe 3 times a day) to pause for 3 minutes? Imagine sinking down inside yourself from your head space to your soul space. Allow yourself to simply rest there. As you do, notice how your energy and mood shifts. This is where the healing happens because your body, mind and spirit are aching to rest. In that rest, you heal all those around you.

Daisy's Devotions
WEEK 23

I'm glad I'm not a scaredy cat. Well, most of the time, I'm not. (My person tells me whenever I say I'm not something, I'm just avoiding that which I am. She calls it Shadow Work and she said it changed her life, but I don't have a clue what the heck she's talking about.)

Anyway, if I hadn't entered this cool doghouse, I wouldn't have allowed myself to be adventurous, fearless, and curious. At least this is what my person is trying to help me understand.

She says exploring new places turns into exploring myself. When I explore myself, I retrieve things that I never knew. Even though I'm not a retriever, I sure like acting like one!

I guess I'm a bit nosy, as I keep sniffing around at my life of discovery. I have a new awareness of how much more often my tail wags because I'm having more fun!

There's zero reason to be gun-shy!

May you discover something new about yourself through adventure, fearlessness, and curiosity!

Your Weekly Treat

When I ask my clients to recall the last time they were adventurous and had fun, the majority can't remember. They share the reasons why, which they discover, are based in fear. "If I schedule time for fun and adventure, then something else will be compromised. The cost might be too high. I don't deserve it."

They don't even allow themselves to come close to exploring a new doghouse like Daisy did here.

How about you? When was the last time you stepped outside of your comfort zone to explore and to be curious with yourself or the world? Self-exploration can be as fun as visiting strange places. Wouldn't you like to have your tail wagging more often?

Set an intention this week to cultivate a curiosity of adventure. Consider what that looks like for you as everyone's situation is unique. Might it be taking yourself somewhere new? Meeting someone new? Or might it be making a new commitment to discover parts of yourself that have been waiting to be revealed?

Use your fear! Feel it! Notice what's possible on the other side! Reflect on how, by taking action, your tail will wag incessantly!

Daisy's Devotions
WEEK 24

I like to nest in this room when I want to feel elegant. It makes me feel like a princess instead of a stray from my previous life.

The places we choose to make a den can either have you digging it or not. That's why I choose environments that make me feel footloose and fancy free!

My nose is my toxicity radar. It gets messages from my gut where and where not to go. I can tell if something is rabid by acting on my animal instinct.

May you access your internal radar to determine environments that uphold the best version of yourself.

Your Weekly Treat

Have you heard it said "what you truly seek has always been seeking you?"

The problem is that we allow ourselves to become distracted, and it cuts off the natural software of the soul. When we choose to be present to what our heart most yearns for, we make choices that reflect our heart's desire. We surround ourselves with people, places, and things that leave us feeling empowered, purposeful, and filled with joy.

Notice this week what may need to change in your environment. Your external world reflects your internal world. What might you need to de-clutter? What toxic relationships might you need to address? What distractions are preventing you from accessing the software of your soul and having you feel footloose and fancy free?

Begin the process this week by acting daily in a way that will have you feeling as elegant as Daisy.

Daisy's Devotions
WEEK 25

I kid you not. This is how my person found me sleeping this morning after I sat with her while she watched a heated political debate last night. I didn't understand what was said, but I can assure you I felt the negative, toxic energy happening! My person seemed to be growling and I didn't like the feel of it at all!

Sometimes I need to bury my head in the sand, dirt, or blanket, in order to come back to my "scentses." Good thing I do, because I can't imagine growling all the time. No muzzle for me!

May you find the truth and happiness from quietude, today and every day forward.

Your Weekly Treat

Boundaries are the ticket to freedom. Subjecting ourselves to toxic people, places and things has a negative impact on our bodies, minds, and spirits. My clients have stated repeatedly that they are afraid of setting and maintaining clear boundaries because they don't want to upset anyone or cause a conflict.

By not having healthy boundaries the upset and conflict remains intrinsic. It diminishes your internal flame, resulting in feelings of resentment and powerlessness. Your spirit yearns for you to create an environment that supports your essence; peace, joy, and love.

This week, consider all the ways you allow toxic energy into your life. Where are these toxic energies that you have tolerated up to this point? Who are the toxic people who you allow into your psyche? Reflect on the fear that has prevented you from setting boundaries. Then ask yourself "If I had no fear, what boundaries would I set that would decrease or eliminate negative energy in my life?"

Last, do it! It may cause conflict, and that's ok. It means you are creating change. Congratulate yourself for honoring you!

Daisy's Devotions
WEEK 26

Do you ever feel like you are too much into the weeds? There's so much going on and you don't know which way is the best way out. It's not that the weeds are necessarily bad. There are just too many choices!

Here's what I do when this happens. I back out of all of it. That way I can see the weeds from a distance, and you know what? Everything seems to fall into place, one weed at a time. When I do, often I will find a reward that I would never have seen had I stayed in deep.

It's that easy: Simply step away, because lingering around leaves you with lots of stickers.

May you find your way out of the weeds and notice that very little matters.

Your Weekly Treat

Being in the weeds is most often the result of overwhelm. Know that overwhelm is a choice; an unconscious habit that only leads to more of it!

The antidote of being in the weeds/overwhelm is to have a plan. Without a plan, you have no idea where to start.

Imagine taking a road trip across the country without a GPS or map. It's going to take you a lot longer to get there than if you had a clear plan with specific check points to know that you are headed in the right direction.

This week, notice when you are in the weeds. Consider how often you enter this space of overwhelm. The insight from this alone should motivate you to pause and notice how a plan will shift you into clarity.

Create a personalized GPS. Identify your destination, set some small goals as milestones to help you measure your progress. Break these milestones down into small, achievable steps that you know you can complete each day. Lastly, find a way to be accountable to yourself so you can feel empowered after doing them.

Daisy's Devotions
WEEK 27

I've been wondering why the two-leggeds try to hide parts of themselves they don't like. "My nose is too big. My butt is too big. My arms are saggy."

I thought I'd try to see what it feels like to hide my nose pretending it was unacceptable.

It's so doggedly constricting! It masked and cut off the natural flow of my breath, and it diminishes my senses. This feels so doggone unnatural.

The truth is that I need not hide anything, all parts of me are useful. There's no point in hiding!

Well, unless you spot a skunk.

Stop worrying about your schnoz, your butt, or any part of yourself. Just love it all!

Ok, I've got some serious sniffing to do!

May you love all parts of you so you can love all parts of me.

Your Weekly Treat

What do you deem unacceptable about yourself and how do you try to hide it? Notice the energy you have given this part or parts of yourself most of your life.

If you are ready to love these parts of you, then write a letter to the unacceptable parts, asking these parts for their forgiveness. Tell these parts about all the ways and reasons why you've made them wrong, and judged them.

Then have them write back to you about how they simply want to be loved and accepted. Have them tell you what they need from you to feel loved. Take the necessary action to gain their love back.

Miracles will happen.

Daisy's Devotions
WEEK 28

My persons tells me evolution is a thing; that you are more evolved than me.

My simple mind questions the above. How is it that you are more evolved when I'm the one who:

Loves unconditionally . . . all the time.

I know there's much more to prove my point, but wait! I'm a dog, so I don't need to prove my point. Getting a treat is way more fun than proving a point.

Maybe though, you could act as if I were more evolved than you. I could teach you lots of things, including how to heel, sense and chill out!

Just chew on this for a while.

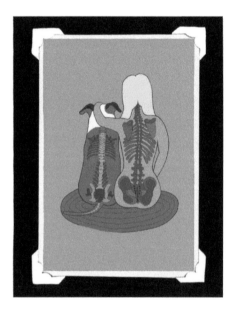

May you act, think, and love unconditionally like a dog.

Your Weekly Treat

Dogs are devoted to their owners because the owners protect and provide for them, just as their packs do in the wild. No matter what, they are there for each other. No judgments, no grudges; just sheer devotion towards each other.

What a tall order for us to live by! How might you let go of the past? How might your life be different if you no longer carried any grudges towards anyone including yourself? You must first believe this is possible, and then you must be willing to be 100% responsible for your thoughts about the past.

This week take a deep dive into your past, reflecting on how you are denying yourself and others of your unconditional love. What righteous position, judgment or belief are you holding onto? Notice the behaviors you have engaged in that have limited you from giving and receiving love.

Write these judgments down on a small piece of paper and then find a safe place to light them up with a match. Take in some deep breaths as you let go of it all. Release yourself and others from the bondage of the narrative of your past.

Then take at least one action that will have you express the love that's waiting to be expressed. If it's scary, that's a good thing!

Daisy's Devotions
WEEK 29

Yeah, this is the result of the fun I had in the river, swimming and chewing up logs. Apparently, I got carried away and ended up swallowing some of what I chewed.

I guess everything has a downside and when you are feeling the effects, it seems like forever.

Now I'm back to my silly and playful self, realizing that everything is temporary.

When your tummy hurts like mine did, remember that this too shall pass.

Or when your heart hurts like my person's does sometimes, I tell her the same thing: This too shall pass.

Trust the downside of your life will get pooped out at some time or another.

May you rest in the knowing that pain is not what blocks the path; it IS the path and your faithful teacher.

Your Weekly Treat

I know when I'm in pain my first reaction is to find a way to eliminate it. The more I try, the worse it gets. The same holds true when I'm suffering mentally and emotionally. It feels permanent, which makes the pain worse.

No one ever said: "Oh, yay! I'm in pain today! Bring it on!" We don't have to be happy about suffering, but we can befriend it. You've heard it said "pain is inevitable and suffering is optional."

What if you allowed yourself to hold your pain from a mindset of allowing, versus managing or controlling? Instead of trying to numb yourself from the uncomfortable feelings, what if you invited it in?

Simply said, what you resist, persists. Daisy does nothing to try to make her pain go away. She allows it, knowing that at times she is completely helpless. Yet she trusts in the process, just as you trust that the seasons change on their own.

This week commit to using your pain instead of it using you. Example: if you have back or neck pain; take some time out and sit with the pain. Bring your attention to the area of your body that hurts. Imagine sending breath to this area, allowing it to be just as it is. As you do, you will notice a shift. The pain may lesson, disappear, or it may still be there, but your kindness creates a softening in your spirit. Do the same for any mental or emotional pain you are experiencing. It takes practice and like anything, the more you do, the less you will suffer.

Daisy's Devotions
WEEK 30

Well, I did it! With a little bit of nudging from my person coaching me, I learned how to respond instead of react. It was so hard for me not to chase these ducks! They looked so inviting! It could have been fun! And then I stopped myself (after feeling a tug on my harness) and noticed that if I had chased them, I would have made the whole experience about me. Instead, I decided to let the ducks enjoy the peace they were experiencing in that moment . . . and then I felt it too!

Those natural instincts can be a bitch, and they don't have to inform what I do anymore.

I'm learning so much from my person, especially since I signed up for an unlimited coaching package that will cover the rest of my life. A little nudge on your harness can go a long way.

What ducks might you want to respond to instead of react?

May you have the awareness to respond to your triggers that will allow you to make the best choices for the highest good.

Your Weekly Treat

When something as inviting as chasing ducks happen in our lives, there's a physiological reaction happening in our bodies. This reaction can be so captivating that we unconsciously act on it. The action may not be in the best interest of ourselves or anyone else.

For me, I can easily react when I see milk chocolate. My mouth begins to water. I get a feeling in my body that has me believe I must have it. I want to react, buy it, and the rest is history. Believe me! If I hadn't learned how to respond versus react, I'd be eating it every day. Now, I pull on my internal harness and remind myself (most of the time) that it's much healthier to walk on by.

What are your triggers? What are the ways that you automatically react? Might it be when someone cuts you off in traffic? Do you react as soon as you see a phone call come in from someone you prefer not to talk to?

Choose one thing in your life that consistently triggers you. Notice how it affects you physically, paying attention to where you feel it in your body. Journal or reflect on how reacting creates a negative impact on yourself and others. Then, make a new commitment to pay attention to the messages in your body when you become triggered, so you can stop and make a new choice.

Daisy's Devotions
WEEK 31

"They" say I have the intelligence of a two-year-old human.

That's all I really need because what's important to two-year olds is: play, kibble, rest, and most of all, being loved. If I'm not loved, I won't thrive.

How about you? Are you getting the love you deserve? Are you thriving?

If not, fetch me. I'll be able to sniff you and know exactly how to help.

Us two-year olds have lots to teach you!

May you be reminded that you are loved and lovable beyond measure.

Your Weekly Treat

I had a client share that she was not capable of loving herself because her mind was consumed with self-judgment and she found herself continually beating herself up. These repetitious thoughts and beliefs blocked any possibilities of being tender and caring towards herself. After coaching her for some time, she learned how to become more mindful, that it was up to her to reprogram her mind. As she did, she began to remember her most child-like self; the lovable, innocent, and worthy part of her. As her mindset shifted, so did her behavior. She gave herself permission to play and have time for herself. As uncomfortable as it was at first to put herself at the top of her list, with practice, she learned to love herself in ways she never imagined.

You can do the same and the first step is to realize all the thoughts, words, and actions that you are currently engaged in that prevent you from feeling self-love. Make a before and after list: On one side of a sheet of paper list all the ways you deny yourself love. On the other side, list all the new thoughts, words, and actions you will take that will cultivate self-love.

Now, commit to one daily self-love practice. Notice how by doing this, magic happens. You will not only have more self-love; you will love others more than you ever thought possible.

Daisy's Devotions
WEEK 32

I learned about this thing called binge watching last night. I pretended I was doing it so I could be close to my person. We were tucked in so close to each other that I could hear her heart beating.

I would choose snuggling any day over a chew toy.

May you always stay close.

Your Weekly Treat

I've yet to meet someone who doesn't want to have close, intimate, relationships. One of the 6 human needs is love/connection. Without it, we fall prey to depression, loneliness, and resignation. However, quite often, we make our issues more important than being in relationship with those we care about. It leaves us feeling unloved and disconnected.

Intimacy happens with vulnerability. Vulnerability is the greatest measurement of courage. Think about it . . . Don't you want your family and friends to be completely transparent and vulnerable with you? If so, the path is for you to model this behavior.

This week, consider one person in your life who you want to feel closer to. Allow yourself to identify the ways you withhold your most authentic self.

Write them a letter, sharing everything you most want them to know. Either send them the letter, or tell them in person. Practice modeling how you want them to be with you. No matter how they respond, you will have created a shift.

Daisy's Devotions
WEEK 33

My person talks to me a lot. I don't know what the words mean, but somehow she communicates in a way that I understand. She tells me that I'm her everything; that when she's not with me, she thinks about me and wants to be with me all the time, that I make her heart melt and I'm her best friend.

From being nobody's anything as a stray, to this, sure makes my tail wag. I hope she knows that she's my everything too. I still don't understand the concept, but I'm understanding the feeling of unconditional love, and I'm totally digging it!

May you be someone's everything.

Your Weekly Treat

I know you know what to do to be someone's everything. "Do unto others as you would have them do unto you," says it all. The more you live this, the more you will be pleased.

Just practice.

Daisy's Devotions
WEEK 34

There's something about being above the ground. My person shared this with me today:

"The sky is above me.

The earth is below me.

And it has me feeling like there's a fire within me.

I'm in the middle."

I don't really care where I am, if I'm safe.

Safety is wherever I am. Safety is wherever you are.

P.S. Being surrounded by pink and green, (the heart chakra) helps too. I'm surrounded in safety and love. I just realized that I'm smart for a dog. I'll have to ask my person to teach me more about the chakras, because it's making scents.

May you be granted protection and safety wherever you may walk and take refuge in the divine wisdom that resides within you.

Your Weekly Treat

The truth is that there are circumstances which are clearly not safe. I have no desire to stand in the middle of an expressway, knowing my chances of being run over are great. There may be some people in your life who you don't feel safe with. To be your most authentic self can make you vulnerable for attack.

Yet there are circumstances and situations in our lives where we can create safety for ourselves. Beliefs and assumptions hinder a feeling of safety.

Carol is a director in a successful corporation who didn't feel safe when meeting with her supervisor for fear of saying something wrong. She believed that if she used her voice by asking for what she needed and offering constructive feedback, she would be fired.

Coaching her to let go of her assumptions and do it anyway resulted in her supervisor being impressed with her new level of leadership. Now she feels proud of herself, and more importantly, she feels safe being transparent and direct.

Where in your life are you not feeling safe because of your beliefs and assumptions? What might be possible by letting them go?

Who is it you want to feel safe with? Go for it this week! Be your most fully expressed self. You'll amaze yourself. Safety is there for you to grasp!

Daisy's Devotions
WEEK 35

Guess what? I LOVE to stare at the bathtub. I haven't figured out why and neither has my person, but I think the bathtub is frickin AWESOME!

My person isn't really into the bathtub like I am, but I find her regularly doing the same thing when she stares out into nature, or the sky, her meal, an insect, or even at me. She's in awe with even the simplest things, just like I am with the bathtub and sometimes my chew toys.
Life is AWE-some and it just seems like things would be better for all of us if we all chose to pawz and be in AWE, even if it's a bathtub.
If you'd like, come on over. I'll show you my AWE-some bathtub.

May you stand in what's before you with awe and be amazed and grateful for the simplest of things.

May you stand in what's before you with awe and be amazed and grateful for the simplest of things.

Your Weekly Treat

I can't imagine my life without a meditation practice of some sort. Without it, I am less mindful, and I miss out of being present in the moment, which is the only way you can experience awe.

However, what I hear from so many people is they are not capable of meditating. They say they can't stop thinking. Meditation is not about stopping all thoughts. Instead, it offers an experience of simply observing one's thoughts versus being engaged in them.

Meditation comes in many forms. Painting, walking in nature, dancing ~ or in Daisy's case, simply staring at an object ~ all are meditations. Any activity, (or non-activity) where you can become more focused is a meditation. THIS is how you experience awe.

This week, find a way that you can spend as little as 10 minutes per day when you can step away from your regular activities. Use this time to notice, observe, and have a quality of wonder and awe.

Awe is right before you. Embrace it, even if it's in the bathtub!

Daisy's Devotions
WEEK 36

I bet when you looked at this photo, your attention was drawn to me; my sweet face and my beautiful markings. Maybe you think I'm cute.

And I bet you didn't question which step I was standing on. You didn't care if I was one step higher, or even at the highest step. You know why? Because it doesn't matter if I'm standing on the lowest or the highest step. What's important is that I'm standing!

You see, dogs don't know how to compare and measure like you do. I like it this way because I don't have to worry about where I need to be in my life, as long as I get chew toys!

Why not try being like me and just be happy wherever you are? I know you can be trainable like I am, so dig into all those ways you compare, and then let this be your season of shedding it all away!

May you grant yourself the wisdom that the highest expression of you is not one step up or one step down. It's right where you are standing now.

Your Weekly Treat

"When I get that promotion, I'll be happier." "When I lose this next 10 pounds, then I'll feel sexy." "When I meditate regularly, I'll be enlightened."

Any of these seem familiar? Well, the bad news is by continuing to live in that mindset, you will forever be chasing something you think you need in order to get that feeling. The good news is these feelings are available right now.

Commit to shedding this week. Reflect on all the ways you are waiting for external circumstances to change your life.

Identify the feelings you've been chasing such as; confidence, accomplishment, connection. Since all these feelings are available in the moment, spend five minutes each day, closing your eyes and accessing the feelings. This is simply about remembering that you are at choice in any given moment to cultivate the experience you desire.

No more chasing. It's right here!

Daisy's Devotions
WEEK 37

Ever find yourself half way in/half way out?

Unlike the two-leggeds, I don't get all squirrelly with being in ambiguity. I mean, it's more fun. You get to experience both in and out; the warm sun and the cool shade.

My person told me she trains people to let go of being so gun-shy with ambiguity. She tells me humans have this need to have all the answers because it gives them a feeling of control.

That would feel like being in a kennel round the clock!

Anyway, you should try sitting underneath a chair like I do and see how much fun it is to be half in and half out!

May you release the need to know and bask in the mystery of life.

Your Weekly Treat

What might your life be like if you completely let go of any need to have answers? How much more emotional and mental space might be freed up by doing so? What is it costing you in terms of peace and joy by being attached to finding answers?

If you think about it, knowing is the booby prize. Once we think we know something, there is no longer a mystery or opportunity to be in inquiry.

This week, choose someone who might be willing to have a conversation around the need to know. Share with them how it hinders you from having peace of mind. Tell them how your experience of life may be different by being in the dark and the light at the same time. Then invite them to share the same. Check in with each other several times this week to report the shifts that are happening by living in the mystery.

Daisy's Devotions
WEEK 38

I shed, ok? Call it dust bunnies, dirt, hair, whatever.

But here's the deal. I don't hold on to it. I let it go!

It all gets vacuumed up and thrown out, thanks to my person. I always shed what I don't need. It makes me feel so clean!

You know where I'm going with this, right?

Not to point paws at you, but . . . how about all the dust bunnies, dirt, or maybe fleas that live in your head? Why not shed it off like me?

Think about how crowded, clouded, and dirty it might be in your head, sort of like the muck in this photo.

Shed your muck like I do. Be muckless, like me!

May you cleanse your heart and soul by shedding all that no longer serves you.

Your Weekly Treat

Daisy is hilarious when I vacuum. She loves to chase it as I move about the house, sucking up all the dirt. I enjoy it as well, but in a different way. I love the way the house looks and feels afterwards. I play a mental game with myself when I'm vacuuming. As I go into each room, I make believe that the dirt, dust bunnies, and hair represent all the crazy thoughts in my head that I've collected over the years that need to be sucked out and removed. I know it sounds silly, but it creates sort of a meditative experience which leaves me feeling cleansed inside and out.

Why not try it this week? Get your vacuum out and do the same thing. If not a vacuum, then use a broom to sweep it all up! When you empty your container, get present to all those thoughts you are letting go of. Have fun with it!

Daisy's Devotions
WEEK 39

Check out my bedroom. It's all mine and I love having my own space.

Us dogs get blamed for having separation anxiety. Well, you might want to pawz for a moment and notice how you might have separation anxiety.

Just because I'm a dog doesn't mean I don't notice. Some of you are overly dependent on others in a way that doesn't look too healthy to me.

It looks like you are trying to fetch something that you already have within yourself. It's like you are constantly begging and pawing at someone to get some sort of treat from them. Instead of being like an annoying flea, try going into your crate every so often. I think my person loves me even more when I do.

Then when we are together, I get so much love, snuggles, kisses, and TREATS!

May you release the fear of abandonment and rest in the knowing that you are never alone.

Your Weekly Treat

We all have a longing for belonging. It gives us a feeling of security. We are designed this way and it's healthy, unless you become overly dependent on others to give you what you can cultivate within yourself.

I dated someone several years ago who could not be happy unless I was with him constantly. His need to always be at my side began to really annoy me. I felt suffocated. I knew it wasn't my job to care-take him in this way.

Clearly, he was seeking something from me that he was unable to generate within himself, which was to believe in himself.

This week reflect on who you might be overly dependent on to meet your needs. Then, have a conversation with the person/s who you most need to be less dependent on. Ask them what it feels like for them. Request they support you in becoming more independent. Then take the necessary actions to create space for both of you. It only gets better from here!

Daisy's Devotions
WEEK 40

"I know there's a mouse under the oven. I just know it. I can smell it. I sense it. I'm not leaving this spot until I catch it. Wait, what will I do with it? What's having me obsess over this? It's starting to make me crazy! I'm spending too much time on something that doesn't matter."

"If I had an ego, my ego would have me wanting to catch the mouse to impress my person. What a waste, because I don't have to do anything different to impress her."

"I'm so done with this. Going back to better things like curling up in my bed."

Learn from me: forget about the mice. Forget about anything that has you obsess. Instead, do anything and everything that feels good! That's what matters most!

May you harness the quality of self-control and be comforted in the stillness and calm.

Your Weekly Treat

Can you think of times when you were so enthralled with something so much that you couldn't think of anything else? You were so determined to get the result you wanted and later realized it didn't matter.

My client, Samantha, was planning a trip for herself and her husband. She was so anxious and frustrated with making sure every day had a scheduled activity, that the logistics were ideal, and that everything was perfectly in order.

She just wanted the two of them to get the most out of every moment of their vacation.

Once they arrived, she began to realize that all the planning and obsessing on making it a perfect trip really didn't matter. They went on a few of the excursions she chose, but found out that doing nothing and spending quality time together was more important.

This week, practice letting go of the things that don't matter. Does it really matter if your gas tank is not completely full, or if the dishes are put away? Does it truly matter that the grass gets cut today?

By letting go of those little things that cause you stress, you'll realize what matters most in every moment.

Daisy's Devotions
WEEK 41

A rainy, gray day. I don't get my person. She craves sunshine and warm weather. The only thing I crave is food, sleep, and water. I wish she could be like me in that way. I don't understand how her brain works. I like how my brain works better because I'm not affected like she is from outside stuff. Things are just the way they are and none of it really matters. And no matter what, you can always play!

Ok, back to my toys.

I'd really like to know how you play, even when things are gray.

May you trust in every moment that life can be as simple as breathing, and as natural as gazing into your loved one's eyes.

Your Weekly Treat

Life can be simple. We can be masterful at creating our own chaos, even when things are going well. Might we be addicted to chaos and not even know it?

It's been a challenge for me to believe that I can be just as happy when it's cloudy, damp, and rainy as when it's sunny and warm. I've realized I've been unconsciously committed to being sad on those dreary days. Where did I learn this? I haven't a clue. What's more important to me is that I adopt Daisy's perspective. When I do, the weather doesn't matter.

What belief or thought have you been unconsciously committed to which causes you discontent? By eliminating these thoughts, how might your life change? How many more days of happiness might you experience?

This week, be like Daisy, and notice how simple life can be.

Daisy's Devotions
WEEK 42

The sun, the shade. Look at how I'm sitting in both. I really have no preference because I have no internal chitter chat about either. I embrace both because there really is no meaning to make about the light versus the dark. It seems that humans are always trying to escape the dark and fetch more light. The real treat is letting go of chasing.

If you let it go, you'll furrever be free like me!

May you be guided into the wisdom that a great light will be available by walking in the darkness.

Your Weekly Treat

Just as a child feels safe with a night light, we can create that safety by allowing ourselves to shine a soft light on the darkness in our lives.

Yet you must be willing to be in the dark to "lighten up." Somehow, as adults, we have been conditioned to avoid the dark. "Shadow work" is a process of discovering parts of yourself that you've been hiding. Once revealed, you have a choice to express characteristics about yourself which have been hidden.

Thinking you are unlovable is a shadow belief. Once you shed light on the truth that you are lovable, you will attract loving relationships. It's a simple shift in perception!

Make a commitment this week to be completely honest with yourself. Ask yourself: "What beliefs must I let go of to experience self-love?" Then share your insights with someone you trust. Ask for their feedback and support.

Daisy's Devotions
WEEK 43

Might you be forgetting that there's always a higher perspective available to you?

In order to access the higher perspective, you must be willing to stand tall and look outside of yourself. You will be amazed by what you can see and learn.

There's so much more to bark about, so stand up tall today and use all your senses to experience more of life. I'm loving every moment and seeing so much more up here because of it! Plus, up here I get to feel what's it's like to be a two legged.

May you be reminded that there are always higher perspectives.

Your Weekly Treat

It's quite difficult to view various perspectives if we are emotionally affected by something or someone. So, the first step is to pause until you are less triggered so you can make a sound decision.

This week, reflect on an upcoming decision that awaits you. What might be your default mode answer? What might be your answer by looking at it from your guru's point of view? Or a loved one's point of view? Or maybe even an adversary's point of view? Imagine you are looking down at your situation from 10,000 feet up and listen for the answers.

I can assure you, possibilities and ideas will be revealed, allowing you to feel empowered over choices that you may never had considered in the past.

My favorite question to ask myself in times of doubt is "What Would (fill in the blank) do?" I always receive impactful wisdom and answers, and I know you will too.

Daisy's Devotions
WEEK 44

Sometimes I really do feel like a queen. It's ok that I think highly of myself. I honor my strengths AND my weaknesses, and I love myself even when I do something like bark too much and end up in the doghouse.

I'm the queen of my universe. Are you the queen or king of yours? If not, you might want to try sniffing and digging around in your life to see what's in the way.

May you treat yourself like royalty and be an example of self-honor, valor, and worthiness.

Your Weekly Treat

This is the week to practice placing yourself on the top of your list. This doesn't mean blowing off your responsibilities. It's about treating yourself the same way you would treat someone you most look up to. Imagine having Jesus or the Buddha as a house guest. How would you treat them? This is how you get to start treating yourself; just like Daisy, as she sits on her "throne" in this photo.

Every day this week, make your usual list of to-do's and make sure you include at least one item on your list with something that will make you feel like royalty. Make sure you set enough time aside to take this action. Don't let anyone or anything get in the way!

Daisy's Devotions
WEEK 45

I'm learning not everything is about me.

This morning I didn't get to go swimming. We went on a boring walk and I wasn't happy. I just want to swim.

My person reminded me that she needs to schedule her time with me in between clients and there wasn't enough time for swimming today. I tried brown nosing her but it didn't work. Total bummer.

I guess relationships need to be a give and take kind of thing. I can't have it all my way all the time.

You might want to consider how you might be making everything all about you. Maybe share your bone with a loved one instead of hogging it all to yourself.

Here's the silver lining from not being able to swim this morning. I got to spoon with my person and that's our favorite thing to do!

May you find a natural cycle of give and take, just as you breathe in and out.

Your Weekly Treat

Do you remember throwing a tantrum as a child because you didn't get something you wanted? You did whatever you could to get your way and it didn't work.

How might that child still be acting out today? What do your tantrums look like? Is it manipulation until someone gives in to you? Is it bribery? Or do you punish someone with silence until you get what you want?

Tantrums, trying to control, and having things all go our way are all coping mechanisms to feel valued and loved.

This week, reflect on how that childlike part of you still wants everything to be your way. Journal about how this negatively impacts your relationships. Then spend more time journaling about where that behavior came from and what need you've been chasing by having things your way.

Have the intention to explore something new about yourself. The wisdom is there if you allow yourself to "drop in" and discover what needs to shift. I trust you will get the answers you need.

Make a commitment to find the balance of give and take.

Daisy's Devotions
WEEK 46

My person is looking at this photo feeling sad because she knows I won't be able to get back into the water until next summer. She thinks that I might get depressed during the dark, bitter cold days having to be shut in.

I'm looking at the photo feeling happy! I have ZERO worries about the winter months. You know why? Because it doesn't matter! Everything is exactly as it should be!

Who knows? I may never swim again and I'm not one bit worried.

I'm giving my person an assignment today: to not worry about anything. Nada, zilch. If she succeeds, I'm going to give her the bone I've been hiding as her reward.

By the way, I have a good feeling I'll be dog paddling sooner than later!

May you throw your worries aside and swim towards joy and gratitude every day.

Your Weekly Treat

My late teacher, Debbie Ford, wrote a book: "The Right Questions". One of the right questions she offers is: "Are you looking at what's right or are you looking at what's wrong?"

Daisy is training me to look at what's right. When I'm looking at what's wrong, like dreading the winter months, already deciding they are going to be horrible, my mind will manifest that exact experience. What if, instead, I chose to look at what's right about the winter? It's a time to sit by a fire, wear soft and cozy sweats, eat comfort food, cross country ski! That puts me in a totally different mood.

You see, whatever we choose to believe, we are 100% committed to that belief, so why not choose what's right about your life?

This week, choose one aspect of your life where you make it a pattern of looking at what's wrong. Notice how it makes you feel. Consider all the new thoughts that can have you see what's right. Write them down, or say them aloud every day. Be patient with yourself, because it takes time to re-wire the brain. With committed effort of looking at what's right your stress level will decrease, and your experience of life will be grounded in the truth.

Daisy's Devotions
WEEK 47

I can run, but I can't hide.

I mean, really. Look at this picture. Isn't it a bit ridiculous? You know I'm a dog behind the covering.

Why is it that humans try to hide so many parts of themselves? The truth is that people know who you are underneath your cover. Why would you chain yourself up like this? I'd feel like I was wearing a choke collar 24/7!

I can't imagine living any other way than showing my raw nakedness. I know it's why my species is so doggedly and irresistibly lovable.

May you remove your veil of illusion and enjoy being irresistibly lovable in your raw nakedness.

Your Weekly Treat

1. What if you chose to show the world the total you; The you who doesn't hide one thing about yourself?

2. Do you know why we hide? We are ashamed of ourselves. Shame comes from self-judgment; believing you are wrong. In her book, Return to Love, Marianne Williamson states: "You are a child of God. Your playing small does not serve the world. There is nothing enlightened about shrinking so that other people won't feel insecure around you. We are all meant to shine, as children do."

The way to shine is to allow your light to shine. Your light shines it's brightest when you eliminate shame and allow yourself to be completely vulnerable, transparent, and authentic. Imagine the implications of this for you! Imagine how much more connected others will feel towards you. Imagine the freedom you will give yourself.

Create a "Shame Buster" this week. You can do a vision board showing how you will be showing up in the world, places you will be going and activities you will be engaging in by being completely shameless. This is a fun and insightful exercise.

Shame is the barrier. Freedom awaits you.

Daisy's Devotions
WEEK 48

This is Paul. Paul fixes things. I just met him today and fell in love with him within minutes. Plus, I could smell his dog on him, so I knew he would like me too.

So, I just threw Paul a bone by just sitting there, (after sniffing him and his toolbox).

My person says the greatest gift you can give someone is your full presence, so I took her advice and pretended I was Paul's apprentice and watched.

What's the point, you ask? Well, the result was: 1. It made my person's heart melt seeing me watch Paul. 2. I know Paul liked it too. 3. I loved being with him.

I guess I did help after all!

May you be the container of presence and melt the hearts of the world.

Your Weekly Treat

Marshall B. Rosenberg, says "Your presence is the most precious gift you can give to another human being."

You don't even have to say anything. Simply be with someone. You will both be greatly rewarded.

Daisy's Devotions
WEEK 49

I bet you might be thinking that I look like I wish I were outside, right? Well, if so, you are barking up the wrong tree. I'm simply taking in the beauty of the outdoors; not necessarily trying to dig anything up. There's really no need to be in any one place. Of course, I love running free in a field or traipsing through the woods, but I am just as happy right here.

I kind of wonder what it's like for you to always be wanting something different in order to be happy.

My person tells me you guys are conditioned to living in scarcity; never having enough and never being enough. Sounds to me like that's a chase you will never reach!

Wherever I am, it is enough. Whatever I have, it is enough. Whoever I am, I am enough, so doggone it, take it from this pooch and try being ok with everything just as it is!

May you find peace no matter where you are, knowing that you are enough.

Your Weekly Treat

I often ask my clients what their definition of "enough" might be. They rarely have an answer. What if the grass is just as green as it needs to be, no matter what side you are on? What if you could fall in love with where you are?

Our ego believes there is a "correct" version of each moment. Living this lie is exhausting! Imagine no longer having an urge to be outside or inside or any "correct" place?

These things that we continue to seek so our ego feels right will never abandon you. Oh, the elation one can feel by setting the ego aside and resting in the soul!

Meditate daily this week. Imagine taking an eighteen-inch journey from your head to your heart. Allow yourself to rest in your heart space, just practicing feeling what's there, without feeling as though you need to correct your experience.

Commit to spending less time in the head and sinking down into your heart and soul space. A mere 5-10 minutes a day is all you need.

Daisy's Devotions
WEEK 50

I have no idea what these guys are doing outside. You see, I don›t get caught up in figuring things out. The «why» really doesn›t matter most of the time.

If I had gotten all wrapped up in trying to figure out what was happening, I wouldn't have enjoyed spying on them so much.

My person helps people to understand being stuck in the "why" of their life can often be a form of escapism. She says it can be an avoidance mechanism that hinders one from enjoying the moment. I think she calls it analysis paralysis.

What if, for just one day, you pretend you have a doggy brain like me. No figuring out anything. No analysis, dissecting. I mean, seriously, the "why" doesn't matter. Just be in the "what."

May you lose your mind and travel into your body to have a heightened experience of the senses in everything you do.

Your Weekly Treat

Carla sought out my coaching because she felt stuck. She needed answers to all the "why's" in her life. "Why did so and so do this to me? Why did I respond so terribly? Why is this happening to me?"

Understanding ourselves and our past is part of our transformational journey, however, being stuck in the "why's" can be an avoidance tactic from moving forward.

Even if she had all her questions answered about her past, it wouldn't change her current situation. Carla started to notice how these "why's" were preventing her from taking charge of her life.

I often ask the question, "If you let go of needing to have the answers, how might you use this energy towards your vision?"

How might you be attached to having answers; answers that won't change your future? Spend some time considering what new actions you can take by letting go of figuring out the past. Let go of the "why's" and let in the "what's." Then make the "what's" happen.

Daisy's Devotions
WEEK 51

I bet you chew your bones like I do. You instinctively adjust your angle to get to the marrow.

My person likes to envision her life as chewing on a bone this way. She likes to practice using her instincts to view her life from all angles. She says it provides her with more marrow than she ever imagined as she flexes and twists the angle of her life this way and that.

It's just like when I hear a strange noise and I tilt my head a bit. My person says it's cute, but she needs to know I do it for a purpose. It helps me retrieve the marrow of the sounds I'm hearing.

May you enjoy the marrow of your life as you open your heart and soul to the perspectives that await the full expression of you.

Your Weekly Treat

It takes a minimum of 300 repetitions to learn a new habit and 3000 repetitions for it to become a natural response.

I love the game of golf. I was struggling with my game for quite some time, so I took some lessons.

I found it so difficult to swing the club in a new way. I had to allow my mind to twist and turn, gripping the club in a whole new way. It felt so unfamiliar and awkward. Yet I knew my game would never improve if I didn't allow myself to see my grip and swing from a new perspective.

It took me more than 300 swings at the driving range for it to feel anywhere close to comfortable and 3000 repetitions to start playing better.

What area of your life is yearning for a perspective shift? How might you adjust your grip in order to see another point of view? Create a 300-repetition discipline that will instill a twist and turn perspective.

You will extract so much more marrow!

Daisy's Devotions
WEEK 52

How often do you find yourself not knowing which path to choose? When I was homeless and living in the streets, I got lost several times.

Guess what? I learned there really are no wrong turns. I just trust my gut and it always directs me to exactly where I want to go. It's no big deal if I get lost because I get to discover beautiful, unexpected paths. And those unexpected paths are exactly where I find myself.

Here's the icing on the cake: Had I not trusted my doggy gut; I never would have landed in a shelter. After several months of being in that lonely doghouse, the love of my life showed up and we are living happily ever after!

May you allow yourself to get lost in the path that takes you to nowhere so you, too, will live happily ever after.

Your Weekly Treat

"Should I go this way? Or that way? Ugh, I can't decide! What if I go the wrong way?"

I know I've been in that mental narrative and it's so emotionally debilitating! It's fear based and I'm not trusting in my instincts like Daisy does.

The truth is sometimes we do go down what we consider the wrong path. But what if you could trust that no matter your choice, the path you chose is exactly the one that offers you an opportunity to enjoy what's in front of you?

Instead of telling yourself, "Damn, I shouldn't have done that," you say to yourself, "This was not what I planned, but I'm going to trust this is exactly where I need to be."

This week, look at all the ways in which you live in self-doubt. Notice your fear of making a "wrong" decision. Then ask yourself my favorite question: "If I had no fear, what would I do?"

Then feel the fear and do it anyway!

Acknowledgements

My love and deep gratitude go, first, to my dog, Daisy.

Needless to say, this book would not have happened without Daisy entering my life. Thank you for being my teacher and for nurturing me into a new expression of love.

To the Animal Care League, for taking Daisy off the streets which kept her from being euthanized so that I could be rescued by her.

To my amazing publisher and dear friend, Jenifer Novak Landers, thank you for your unique, creative mind, your willingness to coach me out of my stuckness during this project, to help me laugh at myself, and for the way you always accept me no matter how I show up.

To Kalyn Block, who edited the manuscript several times with such tenderness and care. Thank you for holding the space for the vision of the book.

For my Facebook friends who suggested I turn this into a book. Without your encouragement, I'd still be wondering whether or not to publish.

To all my spiritual teachers, I offer thanks. For you have taught me how to use my intuition and ability to source the truth.

About the Author

Debbie Leoni is the owner of Being Fearless Coaching where she supports leaders worldwide to shift their fear into fearlessness.

Taught by thought leaders including Deepak Chopra, Debbie Ford and Marianne Williamson, she has become a respected expert in the field of personal growth and spirituality. Whether Debbie is leading Being Fearless workshops, teaching leadership training programs, or coaching individuals and groups, she supports people through their own journey from fear into courage, leading them in a fuller expression of the life they desire.

Debbie is a Master Certified Coach with the International Coach Federation.

She is the author of three other books: "I Am Fearless: Twelve Elements of Fearless Living", "Pure Wealth: 26 Ways to Crazy Profitability" and "Brilliant Breakthroughs for the Small Business Owner".

Debbie lives in Geneva, Illinois with Daisy.

Connect with Daisy!

Join us on Social Media

Facebook:
https://www.facebook.com/beingfearlesscoaching

Instagram:
https://www.instagram.com/debbieleoni

Send us an email:
debbie@debbieleoni.com

Visit our website!
www.debbieleoni.com/books

A Special Thank You

for sponsoring Daisy's Treats

We are proud to introduce you to
"Real Meat Treats and Foods"
Because they are top notch in our book!

Quality in the Bowl

Makers of all-natural 95% meat and poultry jerky treats
and foods for dogs & cats who care what they eat!

Money in Your Pocket!

Quality Meats - Affordable Price.
10%-25% less than our closest competitors!

www.RealMeatPet.co

Sign up for discounts on our website.